AMAZING
FACTS ABOUT
DINOSAURS

MATHEW J. WEDEL

CAPSTONE PRESS
a capstone imprint

COELOPHYSIS

(seel-OH-fie-sis)

TIME PERIOD LIVED: LATE TRIASSIC 235 TO 228 MILLION YEARS AGO

LOCATION: NEW MEXICO AND ARIZONA, USA, AND SOUTH AFRICA

LENGTH: 9.8 FEET (3 M)

More than 1,000 **COELOPHYSIS** skeletons were found in a **SINGLE QUARRY** at Ghost Ranch, New Mexico, USA.

ONE OF THEM HAD THE BONES OF A SMALL CROCODILE INSIDE ITS RIBCAGE—ITS LAST MEAL!

EORAPTOR HAD **HOLLOW** BONES.

EORAPTOR

(EE-oh-RAP-tor)

TIME PERIOD LIVED: LATE TRIASSIC
235 TO 228 MILLION YEARS AGO

LOCATION: ARGENTINA

LENGTH: 3.28 FEET (1 M)

Its hollow bones made it **LIGHTWEIGHT** and **SPEEDY**.

HERRERASAURUS

(herr-ray-rah-SORE-us)

TIME PERIOD LIVED: LATE TRIASSIC
228 MILLION YEARS AGO

LOCATION: ARGENTINA

LENGTH: 9.8 FEET (3 M)

THIS DINOSAUR WALKED ON TWO LEGS AS IT HUNTED.

THREE TOES?

Herrerasaurus had five toes on each foot, but only three reached the ground!

LILIENSTERNUS WAS A FIERCE PREDATOR!

With its **SHARP TEETH** and **CLAWS**, it could easily **ATTACK** and bring down a young **PLATEOSAURUS.**

LILIENSTERNUS

(lil-ee-en-shtern-us)

TIME PERIOD LIVED: **LATE TRIASSIC 235 TO 228 MILLION YEARS AGO**

LOCATION: **ARGENTINA**

LENGTH: **9.8 FEET (3 M)**

5

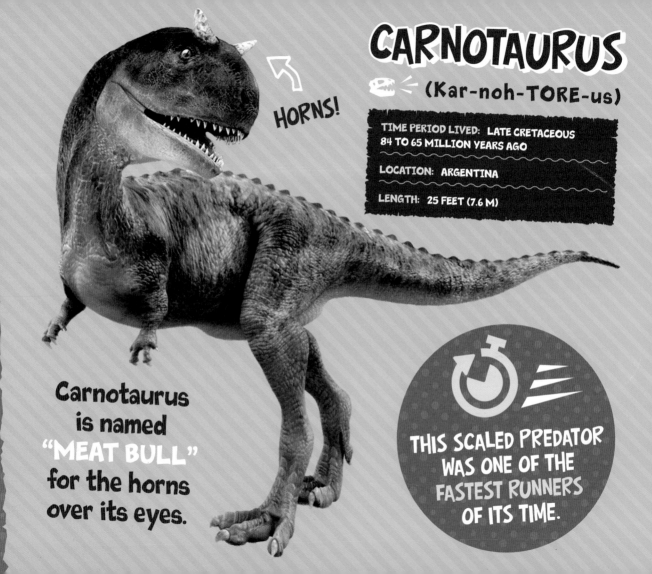

HORNS!

CARNOTAURUS

(Kar-noh-TORE-us)

TIME PERIOD LIVED: LATE CRETACEOUS
84 TO 65 MILLION YEARS AGO

LOCATION: ARGENTINA

LENGTH: 25 FEET (7.6 M)

Carnotaurus
is named
"MEAT BULL"
for the horns
over its eyes.

THIS SCALED PREDATOR
WAS ONE OF THE
FASTEST RUNNERS
OF ITS TIME.

DAHALOKELY

(dah-HAH-loo-KAY-lee)

Dahalokely means "SMALL THIEF" in Malagasy, the native language of Madagasgar.

IT WASN'T VERY BIG— ONLY A LITTLE LARGER THAN A HUMAN.

MASIAKASAURUS

(MAS-ee-ah-ka-SAW-rus)

TIME PERIOD LIVED: LATE CRETACEOUS
72 TO 66 MILLION YEARS AGO

LOCATION: MADAGASGAR

LENGTH: 6.56 FEET (2 M)

MASIAKASAURUS HAD TEETH THAT POINTED FORWARD.

ITS TEETH WERE ABLE TO GRAB SLIPPERY, SQUIRMY PREY SUCH AS FISH AND LIZARDS.

Like many **BUMP-HEADED** meat-eaters, Rugops had **WRINKLED BONES** on its skull.

RUGOPS

(ROO-gops)

TIME PERIOD LIVED: MIDDLE CRETACEOUS 110 TO 93.5 MILLION YEARS AGO

LOCATION: NIGER

LENGTH: 23 FEET (7 M)

RUGOPS MEANS "ROUGH FACE".

BARYONYX

(bah-ree-ON-icks)

TIME PERIOD LIVED: EARLY CRETACEOUS 130 MILLION YEARS AGO

LOCATION: ENGLAND AND SPAIN

LENGTH: 32 FEET (10 M)

This dinosaur was a **SURF** and **TURF** eater! It liked **STEAK** and **SEAFOOD.**

ITS JAWS AND TEETH LOOKED MUCH LIKE THOSE OF TODAY'S CROCODILES.

SPINOSAURUS

 ← (SPINE-oh-SORE-us)

TIME PERIOD LIVED: MIDDLE CRETACEOUS
100 MILLION YEARS AGO

LOCATION: EGYPT AND MOROCCO

LENGTH: 50 FEET (15 M)

Spinosaurus had a **LARGE SAIL** that stood on its **BACK.**

A LONG SNOUT AND **CONE-SHAPED TEETH** HELPED IT CATCH FISH TO EAT.

SUCHOMIMUS

 (SOOCH-oh-MI-mus)

Suchomimus was a **FIERCE** meat-eater with **122 TEETH.**

THAT'S FOUR TIMES AS MANY TEETH AS A HUMAN BEING!

TALL SPINES shot upward from Acrocanthosaurus' **BACK.**

The spines may have formed a **SAIL** or supported a **HUMP OF MUSCLE.**

ACROCANTHOSAURUS
(ah-kroh-kan-tho-SORE-us)

TIME PERIOD LIVED: EARLY CRETACEOUS 110 MILLION YEARS AGO

LOCATION: OKLAHOMA, TEXAS, AND UTAH, USA

LENGTH: 39 FEET (12 M)

SAIL or HUMP OF MUSCLE?

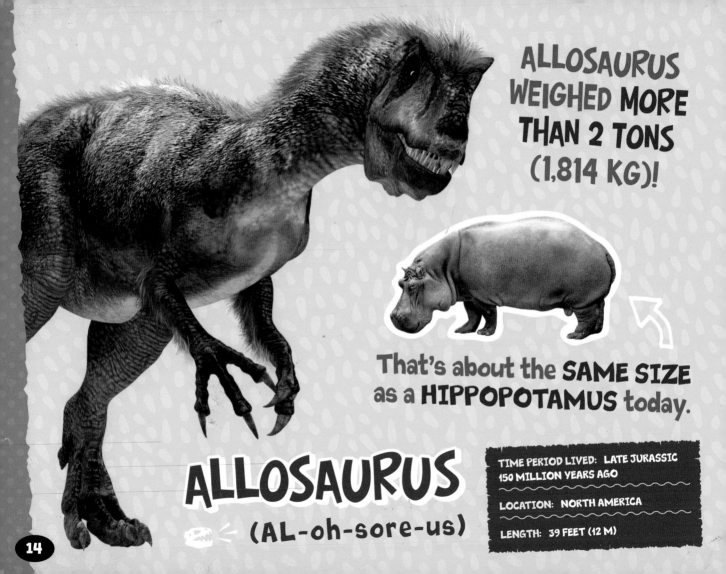

ALLOSAURUS WEIGHED MORE THAN 2 TONS (1,814 KG)!

That's about the **SAME SIZE** as a **HIPPOPOTAMUS** today.

ALLOSAURUS
(AL-oh-sore-us)

TIME PERIOD LIVED: LATE JURASSIC 150 MILLION YEARS AGO

LOCATION: NORTH AMERICA

LENGTH: 39 FEET (12 M)

CARCHARODONTOSAURUS HAD **LARGE TEETH** WITH BUMPS CALLED **SERRATIONS**.

THEY COULD CUT THROUGH MEAT LIKE A STEAK KNIFE!

CARCHARODONTOSAURUS

 (Kar-KARE-o-DON-toe-SORE-us)

TIME PERIOD LIVED: MIDDLE CRETACEOUS 100 MILLION YEARS AGO

LOCATION: ALGERIA, EGYPT, MOROCCO, AND NIGER

LENGTH: 40 FEET (12 M)

Wait, is that a **POMPADOUR?**

NO! Cryolophosaurus had a **SIDEWAYS CREST** on top of its head.

CRYOLOPHOSAURUS
(CRY-o-LOAF-oh-SORE-us)

TIME PERIOD LIVED: EARLY JURASSIC 190 MILLION YEARS AGO

LOCATION: ANTARCTICA

LENGTH: 20 FEET (6 M)

A GIGANOTOSAURUS' SKULL WAS **5 FEET (1.5 M)** LONG.

But its **BRAIN** was only the size of a **BANANA!**

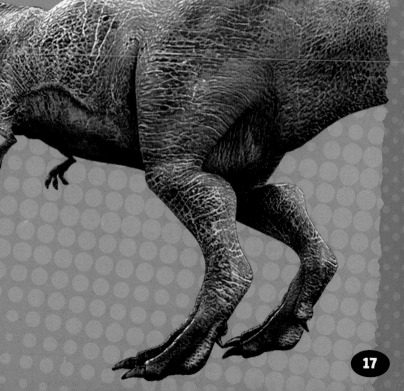

GIGANOTOSAURUS

(gig-an-OH-toe-SORE-us)

TIME PERIOD LIVED: MIDDLE CRETACEOUS
100 MILLION YEARS AGO

LOCATION: ARGENTINA

LENGTH: 41 FEET (12.5 M)

NEOVENATOR

(NEE-uh-ve-NAY-tor)

TIME PERIOD LIVED: EARLY CRETACEOUS
130 MILLION YEARS AGO

LOCATION: ENGLAND

LENGTH: 23 FEET (7 M)

ONE NEOVENATOR SKELETON HAD BROKEN BONES IN ITS TAIL, RIBCAGE, AND SHOULDER.

IT MUST HAVE BROKEN BONES DURING BRUTAL FIGHTS WITH OTHER DINOSAURS.

ALBERTOSAURUS PROBABLY HUNTED IN PACKS.

PALEONTOLOGISTS FOUND A GROUP OF 26 ALBERTOSAURUS INCLUDING GROWN-UPS, TEENAGERS, AND BABIES.

ALBERTOSAURUS

(al-BERT-oh-SORE-us)

TIME PERIOD LIVED: LATE CRETACEOUS 70 MILLION YEARS AGO

LOCATION: MONTANA, USA, AND ALBERTA, CANADA

LENGTH: 28 FEET (8.5 M)

ALIORAMUS

 (al-ee-OH-rah-mus)

TIME PERIOD LIVED: LATE CRETACIOUS 70 MILLION YEARS AGO

LOCATION: MONGOLIA

LENGTH: 19 FEET (5.8 M)

Alioramus had **FIVE HORNS** on top of its snout.

WHAT A SHOW-OFF!

COELURUS

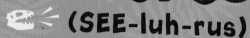 (SEE-luh-rus)

TIME PERIOD LIVED: LATE JURASSIC 155 MILLION YEARS AGO

LOCATION: WYOMING AND UTAH, USA

LENGTH: 8 FEET (2.5 M)

Coelurus had **LONG, THIN FINGERS** and a **LONG TAIL.**

IT WAS A **FAST-RUNNING HUNTER** OF SMALL ANIMALS.

COMPSOGNATHUS

(komp-sog-NAY-thus)

TIME PERIOD LIVED: LATE JURASSIC
150 MILLION YEARS AGO

LOCATION: GERMANY AND FRANCE

LENGTH: 4 FEET (1.2 M)

Compsognathus was a **FAST RUNNER** and hunted **LIZARDS** and **BUGS.**

ONE FOSSIL HAD THE SKELETON OF A LIZARD IN ITS STOMACH.

DASPLETOSAURUS

(da-SPLEET-oh-SORE-us)

TIME PERIOD LIVED: LATE CRETACEOUS 80 MILLION YEARS AGO

LOCATION: MONTANA, NEW MEXICO, USA, AND ALBERTA, CANADA

LENGTH: 30 FEET (9 M)

Daspletosaurus **DID NOT** always get along.

MANY DASPLETOSAURUS FOSSILS HAVE HEALED INJURIES, SHOWING THAT THESE DINOS BIT EACH OTHER'S NOSES!

NOT ALL TYRANNOSAURS WERE GIANTS.

Eotyrannus was about the size of a LARGE DOG today.

EOTYRANNUS

(EE-oh-tie-RAN-us)

TIME PERIOD LIVED: EARLY CRETACEOUS
130 MILLION YEARS AGO

LOCATION: ENGLAND

LENGTH: 15 FEET (4.6 M)

GUANLONG

 (GWAN-long)

TIME PERIOD LIVED: LATE JURASSIC 160 MILLION YEARS AGO

LOCATION: CHINA

LENGTH: 9.8 FEET (3 M)

GUANLONG CAUSED QUITE A "FLAP" WHEN IT WAS DISCOVERED.

IT WAS ONE OF THE FIRST TYRANNOSAURS FOUND WITH FEATHERS!

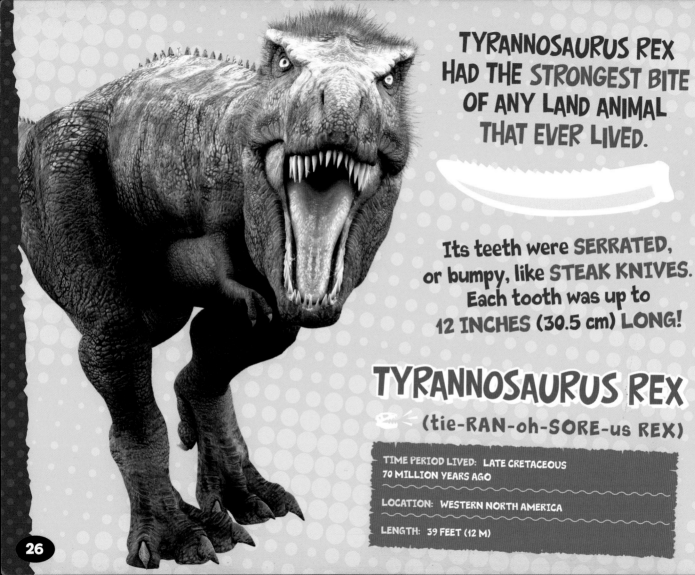

TYRANNOSAURUS REX HAD THE STRONGEST BITE OF ANY LAND ANIMAL THAT EVER LIVED.

Its teeth were SERRATED, or bumpy, like STEAK KNIVES. Each tooth was up to 12 INCHES (30.5 cm) LONG!

TYRANNOSAURUS REX
(tie-RAN-oh-SORE-us REX)

TIME PERIOD LIVED: LATE CRETACEOUS 70 MILLION YEARS AGO

LOCATION: WESTERN NORTH AMERICA

LENGTH: 39 FEET (12 M)

DEINOCHEIRUS

(DINE-oh-KIRE-us)

TIME PERIOD LIVED: LATE CRETACEOUS 71 TO 69 MILLION YEARS AGO

LOCATION: MONGOLIA

LENGTH: 32.8 FEET (10 M)

Deinocheirus had a **DUCKLIKE BILL**, a **SAIL** on its back, and a **HUGE BELLY**.

IT DEFENDED ITSELF WITH BIG CLAWS ON ITS HANDS.

GALLIMIMUS MEANS "CHICKEN MIMIC."

A full-grown Gallimimus weighed **HALF A TON** (454 kg).

THAT'S SOME CHICKEN!

GALLIMIMUS

 (GAL-uh-MY-mus)

TIME PERIOD LIVED: **LATE CRETACEOUS 70 MILLION YEARS AGO**

LOCATION: **MONGOLIA**

LENGTH: **20 FEET (6 M)**

ORNITHOMIMUS

(ORN-ith-oh-MY-mus)

TIME PERIOD LIVED: LATE CRETACEOUS 65 MILLION YEARS AGO

LOCATION: COLORADO, WYOMING, SOUTH DAKOTA, AND UTAH, USA, AND CANADA

LENGTH: 9.8 FEET (3 M)

ORNITHOMIMUS WAS COVERED IN FEATHERS.

It had long, WINGLIKE FEATHERS on its ARMS and a BEAK instead of teeth.

Like a modern mole, tiny Shuvuuia had **SHORT, STRONG ARMS** for **DIGGING.**

BUT SHUVUUIA HAD LONG, LIGHT LEGS FOR RUNNING, LIKE A TODAY'S ROADRUNNER.

SHUVUUIA

(SHOE-vu-YOU-ee-uh)

TIME PERIOD LIVED: LATE CRETACEOUS 86 TO 70 MILLION YEARS AGO

LOCATION: MONGOLIA

LENGTH: 2 FEET (0.6 M)

BAMBIRAPTOR MAY HAVE CLIMBED TREES.

It also may have **CURLED UP BENEATH** its **FEATHERS** to **SLEEP.**

BAMBIRAPTOR

 (BAM-bee-rap-tor)

TIME PERIOD LIVED: LATE CRETACEOUS
75 MILLION YEARS AGO

LOCATION: NORTH AMERICA

LENGTH: 3 FEET (1 M)

BUITRERAPTOR

(BWEE-tree-rap-tor)

TIME PERIOD LIVED: LATE CRETACEOUS 90 MILLION YEARS AGO

LOCATION: ARGENTINA

LENGTH: 4 FEET (1.3 M)

The TINY Buitreraptor only WEIGHED 6 POUNDS (2.7 KG).

THAT'S ABOUT THE SAME AS A CHIHUAHUA TODAY.

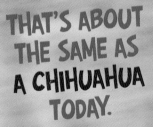

DEINONYCHUS TORE PREY WITH ITS **LONG CLAWS** AND **SHARP TEETH.**

DEINONYCHUS
(die-NON-i-kuss)

TIME PERIOD LIVED: EARLY CRETACEOUS 118 TO 110 MILLION YEARS AGO

LOCATION: UNITED STATES

LENGTH: 9.8 FEET (3 M)

They probably worked together **IN PACKS** to bring down **LARGER DINOSAURS.**

Microraptor had long, **WINGLIKE** feathers on both its **ARMS** and **LEGS**.

IT PROBABLY USED ITS FOUR WINGS TO **JUMP** AND GLIDE FROM **TREE TO TREE**.

MICRORAPTOR

(MIKE-row-rap-tor)

TIME PERIOD LIVED: **EARLY CRETACEOUS 125 TO 122 MILLION YEARS AGO**

LOCATION: **CHINA**

LENGTH: **2.6 FEET (0.8 M)**

TROODON MEANS "WOUNDING TOOTH".

TROODON
(TROW-oh-don)

It had a very **BIG BRAIN** for its size and may have been the **SMARTEST** of all dinosaurs.

TIME PERIOD LIVED: LATE CRETACEOUS 74 TO 65 MILLION YEARS AGO

LOCATION: UNITED STATES AND CANADA

LENGTH: 9.8 FEET (3 M)

VELOCIRAPTOR

(VUH-law-suh-rap-tor)

TIME PERIOD LIVED: LATE CRETACEOUS
75 MILLION YEARS AGO

LOCATION: ASIA

LENGTH: 5.9 FEET (1.8 M)

Velociraptor became popular after being featured in the **JURASSIC PARK** movies.

VELOCIRAPTORS WERE ABOUT THE SIZE OF MODERN TURKEYS.

However, in the movies the **VELOCIRAPTORS** were based on the much larger **DEINONYCHUS** and **UTAHRAPTOR.**

YAVERLANDIA WAS ONE SMART DINO!

It had a **LARGE BRAIN** in its domed head.

YAVERLANDIA

(yah-ver-LAND-ee-ah)

TIME PERIOD LIVED: EARLY CRETACEOUS
130 TO 125 MILLION YEARS AGO

LOCATION: ISLE OF WIGHT IN GREAT BRITAIN

LENGTH: 10 FEET (3 M)

It was so BIRDLIKE that paleontologists mistook it for a BIRD at first.

AVIMIMUS

(ah-vee-MY-mus)

TIME PERIOD LIVED: LATE CRETACEOUS 80 TO 75 MILLION YEARS AGO

LOCATION: CHINA AND MONGOLIA

LENGTH: 4.9 FEET (1.5 M)

FOR PROTECTION AGAINST PREDATORS, AVIMIMUS LIVED IN LARGE HERDS.

BEIPIAOSAURUS

(BAY-pyow-sore-us)

TIME PERIOD LIVED: EARLY CRETACEOUS 127 TO 121 MILLION YEARS AGO

LOCATION: CHINA

LENGTH: 6.7 FEET (2 M)

For a long time, the only dinosaurs found with **FEATHERS** were **TINY** and **VERY BIRDLIKE**.

Beipiaosaurus changed that—it was the size of a **SMALL BEAR**.

The name Caudipteryx means "TAIL WING" or "TAIL FEATHERS".

CAUDIPTERYX
(CAW-dip-TER-iks)

TIME PERIOD LIVED: **EARLY CRETACEOUS 125 TO 122 MILLION YEARS AGO**

LOCATION: **NORTHEASTERN CHINA**

LENGTH: **3.3 FEET (1 M)**

IT WAS THE FIRST DINOSAUR TO BE FOUND WITH A BIG FAN OF TAIL FEATHERS, LIKE A TURKEY TODAY.

FALCARIUS

 (FAL-cuh-REE-us)

TIME PERIOD LIVED: EARLY CRETACEOUS
125 MILLION YEARS AGO

LOCATION: UNITED STATES

LENGTH: 13 FEET (4 M)

FALCARIUS WAS RELATED TO CARNIVORES LIKE ALLOSAURUS AND T. REX.

BUT IT EVOLVED TO EAT PLANTS, NOT MEAT!

INCISIVOSAURUS

(in-SIZE-iv-uh-saw-rus)

INCISIVOSAURUS HAD BIG FRONT TEETH FOR CUTTING PLANTS, LIKE A MODERN BEAVER OR A RABBIT.

Protarchaeopteryx looked a lot like a bird, **BUT IT DIDN'T FLY.**

Long, FEATHERED ARMS extended from its small, feathered body.

PROTARCHAEOPTERYX
(PRO-tark-ee-OP-ter-iks)

TIME PERIOD LIVED: EARLY CRETACEOUS 125 TO 113 MILLION YEARS AGO

LOCATION: CHINA

LENGTH: 6.7 FEET (2 M)

Therizinosaurus had the **LONGEST CLAWS** of any dinosaur.

THEY WERE MORE THAN 3 FEET (0.9 M) LONG!

THERIZINOSAURUS

(THER-ih-zine-oh-sore-us)

TIME PERIOD LIVED: LATE CRETACEOUS 70 MILLION YEARS AGO

LOCATION: MONGOLIA

LENGTH: 3 FEET (0.9 M)

EFRAASIA

(eh-FRAZE-ee-ah)

TIME PERIOD LIVED: LATE TRIASSIC 210 MILLION YEARS AGO

LOCATION: GERMANY AND EUROPE

LENGTH: 20 FEET (6 M)

Efraasia was an **HERBIVORE**— it **ATE PLANTS.**

IT WALKED ON TWO LEGS AND USED ITS FRONT TEETH TO SCRAPE LEAVES FROM TREES.

PLATEOSAURUS

(PLAT-ee-oh-SORE-us)

TIME PERIOD LIVED: LATE TRIASSIC
210 MILLION YEARS AGO

LOCATION: EUROPE

LENGTH: 23-30 FEET (7-9 M)

Sometimes WHOLE HERDS of these heavy dinosaurs would get TRAPPED IN MUD.

PLATEOSAURUS WAS A GIANT! IT WEIGHED UP TO 4 TONS (3,629 KG).

Their skeletons would be preserved and were later DISCOVERED TOGETHER.

Saturnalia had a **LONG TAIL** that it used to **TURN QUICKLY** when running.

LIKE A MODERN IGUANA, IT ATE PLANTS USING ITS LEAF-SHAPED TEETH.

SATURNALIA

(sat-urn-AHL-ee-ah)

TIME PERIOD LIVED: LATE TRIASSIC
225 MILLION YEARS AGO

LOCATION: BRAZIL AND ZIMBABWE

LENGTH: 5 FEET (1.5 M)

THECODONTOSAURUS

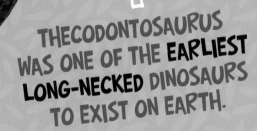 (THEEK-oh-DON-toh-SORE-us)

THECODONTOSAURUS WAS ONE OF THE EARLIEST LONG-NECKED DINOSAURS TO EXIST ON EARTH.

It was also one of the FIRST dinosaurs to be DISCOVERED.

In 1836, it became only the FIFTH dinosaur ever to be NAMED.

APATOSAURUS WEIGHED ABOUT **35 TONS** (32 METRIC TONS)!

APATOSAURUS

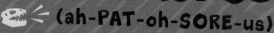 (ah-PAT-oh-SORE-us)

TIME PERIOD LIVED: LATE JURASSIC 150 MILLION YEARS AGO

LOCATION: NORTH AMERICA

LENGTH: 69 FEET (21 M)

That's the weight of about **FIVE** modern **AFRICAN ELEPHANTS!**

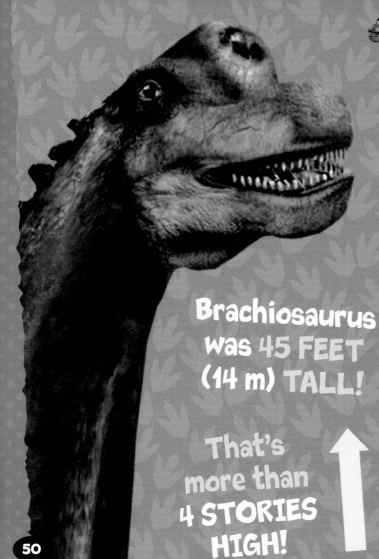

LONG FRONT LEGS HELPED BRACHIOSAURUS EAT LEAVES FROM TALL TREES.

Brachiosaurus was 45 FEET (14 m) TALL!

That's more than 4 STORIES HIGH!

BRACHIOSAURUS
(BRAK-ee-oh-SORE-us)

TIME PERIOD LIVED: LATE JURASSIC 150 MILLION YEARS AGO

LOCATION: NORTH AMERICA

LENGTH: 98 FEET (30 M)

BRACHYTRACHELOPAN

(BRAK-i-TRACH-eh-LOH-pan)

**TIME PERIOD LIVED: LATE JURASSIC
150 MILLION YEARS AGO**

LOCATION: ARGENTINA

LENGTH: 35 FEET (11 M)

Brachytrachelopan
had a built-in WEAPON—
a LONG TAIL it could
use as a WHIP!

ITS NECK WAS JUST
5 FEET (1.5 M) LONG.

CAMARASAURUS

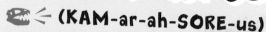 (KAM-ar-ah-SORE-us)

TIME PERIOD LIVED: LATE JURASSIC
150 TO 145 MILLION YEARS AGO

LOCATION: UNITED STATES

LENGTH: 50 FEET (15 M)

SCIENTISTS HAVE FOUND BONES OF A BABY CAMARASAURUS THAT HAD NOT YET HATCHED OUT OF ITS EGG.

DIPLODOCUS

(di-PLAH-di-kus)

TIME PERIOD LIVED: LATE JURASSIC 150 MILLION YEARS AGO

LOCATION: NORTH AMERICA

LENGTH: 90 FEET (27 M)

Diplodocus was one of the **SKINNIEST** large dinosaurs.

It didn't weigh much more than a big **ELEPHANT** today.

HUABEISAURUS

(HOO-ah-bay-SORE-us)

TIME PERIOD LIVED: LATE CRETACEOUS 75 MILLION YEARS AGO

LOCATION: CHINA

LENGTH: 55 FEET (17 M)

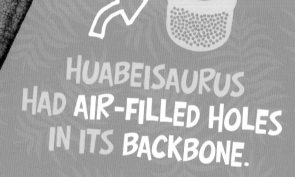

HUABEISAURUS HAD **AIR-FILLED HOLES** IN ITS **BACKBONE.**

The pattern of the **AIR SPACES** helps **SCIENTISTS** tell Huabeisaurus **APART** from its **RELATIVES.**

Omeisaurus' **NECK** was **30 FEET** (9 m) **LONG**.

OMEISAURUS

(OH-mee-sore-us)

TIME PERIOD LIVED: LATE JURASSIC 169 TO 159 MILLION YEARS AGO

LOCATION: CHINA

LENGTH: 30 FEET (9 M)

THAT'S THE LENGTH OF A SMALL HOUSE!

SUUWASSEA

(soo-wah-SEE-uh)

SUUWASSEA'S TEETH WERE SHAPED LIKE PENCILS.

This dinosaur used its TEETH to STRIP BRANCHES of their LEAVES.

56

AMPELOSAURUS HAD BONY ARMOR IN ITS SKIN.

THE LARGEST PIECES OF ARMOR WERE THE SIZE OF DINNER PLATES!

AMPELOSAURUS

◄(AM-pel-oh-SORE-us)

TIME PERIOD LIVED: LATE CRETACEOUS 70 MILLION YEARS AGO

LOCATION: FRANCE

LENGTH: 50 FEET (15 M)

ARGENTINOSAURUS

(AR-gen-teen-oh-SORE-us)

TIME PERIOD LIVED: MIDDLE CRETACEOUS
100 MILLION YEARS AGO

LOCATION: ARGENTINA

LENGTH: 100 FEET (30 M)

ARGENTINOSAURUS IS STILL THE LARGEST KNOWN DINOSAUR.

Its **THIGHBONE** was just over **8 FEET** (2.4 m) LONG!

That's the distance from the **FLOOR TO THE CEILING** in most houses.

FUTALOGNKOSAURUS HAD HIPS ALMOST 10 FEET (3 M) WIDE!

IT ATE TREE LEAVES IN A TROPICAL FOREST.

FUTALOGNKOSAURUS

(FUT-ah-LONG-kuh-SORE-us)

TIME PERIOD LIVED: LATE CRETACEOUS 85 MILLION YEARS AGO

LOCATION: SOUTH AMERICA

LENGTH: 85 FEET (26 M)

MAGYAROSAURUS

 (MAG-ee-ah-ro-sore-us)

TIME PERIOD LIVED: LATE CRETACEOUS
70 MILLION YEARS AGO

LOCATION: ROMANIA

LENGTH: 20 FEET (6 M)

MAGYAROSAURUS HAD BONY PLATES COVERING ITS BACK.

IT WAS THE SMALLEST LONG-NECKED DINOSAUR WITH ARMOR.

Paralititan was one of the **LARGEST DINOSAURS.**

IT WEIGHED
70 TONS
(64 metric tons)!

ITS FOSSIL WAS FOUND IN A MANGROVE SWAMP.

PARALITITAN

(para-lee-tie-TAN)

TIME PERIOD LIVED: MIDDLE CRETACEOUS
95 MILLION YEARS AGO

LOCATION: EGYPT

LENGTH: 100 FEET (30 M)

Saltasaurus was the **FIRST** long-necked dinosaur to be **DISCOVERED** with **ARMOR PLATES.**

SALTASAURUS

 (SALT-ah-sore-us)

TIME PERIOD LIVED: LATE CRETACEOUS 70 TO 65 MILLION YEARS AGO

LOCATION: ARGENTINA

LENGTH: 25 FEET (8 M)

GIGANTSPINOSAURUS

(JIG-ant-spin-oh-SORE-us)

TIME PERIOD LIVED: LATE JURASSIC 160 MILLION YEARS AGO

LOCATION: CHINA

LENGTH: 15 FEET (4.6 M)

GIGANTSPINOSAURUS HAD HUGE SPIKES ON ITS SHOULDERS.

THIS DINO PROBABLY USED ITS SPIKES FOR PROTECTION AND FOR SHOWING OFF.

63

HESPEROSAURUS

(HESP-er-uh-SORE-us)

TIME PERIOD LIVED: LATE JURASSIC
150 MILLION YEARS AGO

LOCATION: WYOMING, USA

LENGTH: 20 FEET (6 M)

WIDE PLATES COVERED HESPEROSAURUS' BACK.

SCIENTISTS USE THE SHAPE OF THE PLATES TO TELL HESPEROSAURUS AND STEGOSAURUS APART.

Like a modern **SPIDER CRAB**, Huayangosaurus had **BONY PLATES** and **SPIKES** for **PROTECTION**.

HUAYANGOSAURUS

← (hoy-YANG-oh-sore-us)

TIME PERIOD LIVED: MIDDLE JURASSIC
165 MILLION YEARS AGO

LOCATION: CHINA

LENGTH: 14.8 FEET (4.5 M)

KENTROSAURUS

(KEN-troh-sore-us)

TIME PERIOD LIVED: LATE JURASSIC
150 MILLION YEARS AGO

LOCATION: TANZANIA

LENGTH: 16 FEET (5 M)

Kentrosaurus had **SMALL PLATES** on its **NECK** and **BODY.**

SPIKES SHOT UP FROM ITS SHOULDERS AND LINED ITS TAIL.

LEXOVISAURUS IS ONE OF THE FEW PLATED DINOSAURS FROM EUROPE.

PALEONTOLOGISTS HAVE FOUND ONLY A FEW OF ITS BONES.

SO NO ONE KNOWS WHAT THIS DINOSAUR LOOKED LIKE.

LEXOVISAURUS
(lex-OH-vi-sore-us)

TIME PERIOD LIVED: MIDDLE JURASSIC 165 MILLION YEARS AGO

LOCATION: ENGLAND AND FRANCE

LENGTH: 5 FEET (1.5 M)

STEGOSAURUS

 (STEG-uh-sore-us)

TIME PERIOD LIVED: LATE JURASSIC
150 MILLION YEARS AGO

LOCATION: NORTH AMERICA

LENGTH: 25 FEET (8 M)

STEGOSAURUS HAD LARGE PLATES POINTING OUT OF ITS BACK.

THE SHARP SPIKES ON ITS TAIL COULD BE USED FOR DEFENSE.

TUOJIANGOSAURUS

 **(too-oh-jian-GO-sore-us)**

TIME PERIOD LIVED: LATE JURASSIC
160 MILLION YEARS AGO

LOCATION: CHINA

LENGTH: 23 FEET (7 M)

Tuojiangosaurus had **NARROW** back plates and **SHARP** shoulder spikes.

Much like a **MODERN PORCUPINE**, Tuojiangosaurus **SCARED OFF** predators with its **SPIKES**.

YINGSHANOSAURUS

(ying-SHAN-oh-sore-us)

TIME PERIOD LIVED: LATE JURASSIC
155 MILLION YEARS AGO

LOCATION: CHINA

LENGTH: 16 FEET (5 M)

Yingshanosaurus had
**VERY SMALL PLATES, only
6 INCHES (15 centimeters) TALL.**

**By comparison,
Stegosaurus' plates were
FOUR TIMES AS BIG!**

THE FIRST DISCOVERED ALETOPELTA DIED AND FLOATED OUT TO SEA.

SHARKS CHOMPED ON ITS BONES.

ALETOPELTA

 (al-ET-oh-pel-tah)

TIME PERIOD LIVED: LATE CRETACEOUS 70 MILLION YEARS AGO

LOCATION: NORTH AMERICA

LENGTH: 16 FEET (5 M)

71

LIKE OTHER ARMORED DINOS, ANKYLOSAURUS HAD PLATES COVERED BY A LAYER OF KERATIN.

Your FINGERNAILS are also made of KERATIN!

ANKYLOSAURUS

(ANK-ih-loh-SORE-us)

TIME PERIOD LIVED: LATE CRETACEOUS 65 MILLION YEARS AGO

LOCATION: NORTH AMERICA

LENGTH: 23 FEET (7 M)

EDMONTONIA HAD **BIG SPIKES** OVER ITS **SHOULDERS** FOR **STABBING** ENEMIES.

EDMONTONIA

(ed-mon-TONE-ee-ah)

TIME PERIOD LIVED: LATE CRETACEOUS 70 MILLION YEARS AGO

LOCATION: MONTANA, USA, AND CANADA

LENGTH: 13 FEET (4 M)

EUOPLOCEPHALUS

(YOU-oh-plo-sef-ah-lus)

Euoplocephalus means "WELL-ARMORED HEAD".

It had a ring of ARMOR around its NECK, like a BONY COLLAR.

TIME PERIOD LIVED: LATE CRETACEOUS 70 MILLION YEARS AGO

LOCATION: WESTERN NORTH AMERICA

LENGTH: 23 FEET (7 M)

THIS DINOSAUR EVEN HAD ARMOR PLATES IN ITS EYELIDS!

GASTONIA

(gas-TOH-nee-ah)

TIME PERIOD LIVED: EARLY CRETACEOUS 129 TO 125 MILLION YEARS AGO

LOCATION: WESTERN NORTH AMERICA

LENGTH: 15 FEET (4.6 M)

Gastonia had TOUGH PLATES and SPIKES on its BODY.

WHEN THREATENED, THIS DINO WOULD CROUCH LOW TO THE GROUND.

Minmi's BACK was PROTECTED with PLATES, and its HIPS and TAIL had SPIKES.

MINMI
(MIN-mee)

TIME PERIOD LIVED: EARLY CRETACEOUS 115 MILLION YEARS AGO

LOCATION: AUSTRALIA

LENGTH: 9.8 FEET (3 M)

IT IS NAMED AFTER MINMI'S CROSSING IN AUSTRALIA.

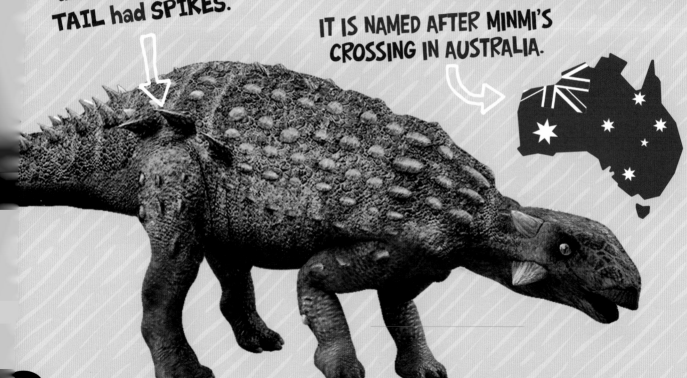

The **BRAIN** of Pawpawsaurus was 4 **INCHES** (10 cm) **LONG** and 1 **INCH** (2.5 cm) **WIDE.**

THAT'S ABOUT THE SIZE OF A PICKLE!

PAWPAWSAURUS

(PAW-paw-sore-us)

TIME PERIOD LIVED: MIDDLE CRETACEOUS
100 MILLION YEARS AGO

LOCATION: TEXAS, USA

LENGTH: 13 FEET (4 M)

POLACANTHUS
(pol-ah-KAN-thus)

TIME PERIOD LIVED: EARLY CREATCEOUS 130 MILLION YEARS AGO

LOCATION: WESTERN EUROPE

LENGTH: 16 FEET (5 M)

POLACANTHUS, FROM ENGLAND, WAS A CLOSE RELATIVE OF GASTONIA, FROM UTAH, USA.

NORTH AMERICA

EUROPE

The ancestors of these dinosaurs walked between **NORTH AMERICA** and **EUROPE** before the **ATLANTIC OCEAN** opened up.

SCUTELLOSAURUS

(sku-TELL-oh-sore-us)

TIME PERIOD LIVED: EARLY JURASSIC
195 MILLION YEARS AGO

LOCATION: ARIZONA, USA

LENGTH: 3.9 FEET (1.2 M)

Scutellosaurus had more than 300 ARMOR PLATES, but it was only about the size of a MODERN DOG!

STRUTHIOSAURUS

(STREW-thee-oh-sore-us)

TIME PERIOD LIVED: LATE CRETACEOUS
65 MILLION YEARS AGO

LOCATION: AUSTRIA, FRANCE, AND ROMANIA

LENGTH: 8.2 FEET (2.5 M)

IT LIVED ON AN ISLAND WITH OTHER DWARF DINOSAURS.

STRUTHIOSAURUS WAS SMALL—ONLY ABOUT THE SIZE OF A MODERN SOFA.

Tiny **GASPARINISAURA** was **ONLY** as **BIG** as a **MODERN CAT!**

But it **LIVED** alongside Argentinosaurus, **THE LARGEST DINOSAUR EVER DISCOVERED.**

GASPARINISAURA

(GAS-pah-rin-ah-sore-ah)

TIME PERIOD LIVED: LATE CRETACEOUS 83 TO 78 MILLION YEARS AGO

LOCATION: ARGENTINA

LENGTH: 2.6 FEET (0.8 M)

Hypsilophodon had **TEETH** that **SLID AGAINST** each other like **SCISSORS.**

The **SLIDING MOTION** kept the teeth **SHARP** for **CUTTING UP** leaves and twigs.

HYPSILOPHODON

(hip-sih-LAH-fah-don)

TIME PERIOD LIVED: **EARLY CRETACEOUS 130 TO 125 MILLION YEARS AGO**

LOCATION: **EUROPE**

LENGTH: **7.5 FEET (2.3 M)**

IGUANODON

(ig-WAH-noh-don)

TIME PERIOD LIVED: EARLY CRETACEOUS
130 MILLION YEARS AGO

LOCATION: EUROPE

LENGTH: 33 FEET (10 M)

THUMB

LIKE OTHER BIRD-FOOT DINOSAURS, IGUANODON HAD LEAF-SHAPED TEETH FOR EATING PLANTS.

ITS HANDS EACH HAD FOUR FINGERS AND A SHARP SPIKE FOR A THUMB.

83

Leaellynasaura had **LARGE EYES** and a **BIG BRAIN**.

Its **TAIL** was **THREE TIMES** as **LONG** as its **BODY!**

LEAELLYNASAURA

(lee-ELL-in-ah-ore-ah)

TIME PERIOD LIVED: EARLY CRETACEOUS 112 TO 104 MILLION YEARS AGO

LOCATION: AUSTRALIA

LENGTH: 3 FEET (1 M)

MUTTABURRASAURUS

🦴 (MUT-ah-burr-ah-SORE-us)

TIME PERIOD LIVED: EARLY CRETACEOUS 112 TO 110 MILLION YEARS AGO

LOCATION: AUSTRALIA

LENGTH: 23 FEET (7 M)

MUTTABURRASAURUS HAD A **BUMP** ON ITS NOSE.

THE BUMP MAY HAVE HAVE BEEN A **BRIGHT COLOR** TO ATTRACT OTHER DINOSAURS.

ORYCTODROMEUS

(or-IK-tow-DROHM-ee-us)

TIME PERIOD LIVED: MIDDLE CRETACEOUS
95 MILLION YEARS AGO

LOCATION: MONTANA, USA

LENGTH: 7 FEET (2.1 M)

ORYCTODROMEUS WAS THE FIRST DINOSAUR DISCOVERED INSIDE A BURROW!

Edmontosaurus had teeth that **LOCKED TOGETHER** to make a **HARD, GRINDING SURFACE.**

The grinding teeth helped Edmontosaurus **CHEW LEAVES** and **FRUITS.**

EDMONTOSAURUS

 (ed-MON-toh-SORE-us)

TIME PERIOD LIVED: LATE CRETACEOUS 70 MILLION YEARS AGO

LOCATION: CANADA AND THE UNITED STATES

LENGTH: 30 FEET (9 M)

HADROSAURUS WAS THE FIRST DINOSAUR DISCOVERED IN NORTH AMERICA.

IT WAS ALSO THE FIRST DINOSAUR TO HAVE ITS SKELETON PUT ON DISPLAY IN A MUSEUM.

HADROSAURUS
(HAD-row-sore-us)

TIME PERIOD LIVED: LATE CRETACEOUS 79 MILLION YEARS AGO

LOCATION: UNITED STATES

LENGTH: 23 FEET (7 M)

FOSSILS of Maiasaura EGGS, YOUNG Maiasaura, and ADULT Maiasaura have been FOUND IN NESTS.

Fossils show that NEWLY-HATCHED Maiasaura COULD NOT WALK right away.

MAIASAURA

(MY-ah-SORE-ah)

TIME PERIOD LIVED: LATE CRETACEOUS 80 TO 75 MILLION YEARS AGO

LOCATION: UNITED STATES

LENGTH: 23 FEET (7 M)

SAUROLOPHUS

(SORE-oh-LOAF-us)

TIME PERIOD LIVED: LATE CRETACEOUS
70 TO 65 MILLION YEARS AGO

LOCATION: MONGOLIA AND CANADA

LENGTH: 27 FEET (8.2 M)

Most duckbills could **BLOW AIR** through their **CRESTS** to make **NOISES.**

But Saurolophus had a crest made of **SOLID BONE.**

SHANTUNGOSAURUS

(shan-TUN-go-sore-us)

TIME PERIOD LIVED: LATE CRETACEOUS
78 TO 74 MILLION YEARS AGO

LOCATION: CHINA

LENGTH: 50 FEET (15.2 M)

SHANTUNGOSAURUS
WAS **LARGER THAN T. REX!**

ITS SKULL WAS MORE THAN 5 FEET (1.5 M) LONG.

TSINTAOSAURUS

(SIN-tao-SORE-us)

TIME PERIOD LIVED: LATE CRETACEOUS 84 TO 71 MILLION YEARS AGO

LOCATION: CHINA

LENGTH: 27 FEET (8.2 M)

The first Tsintaosaurus fossils included a **SKULL** with a **SPIKE** on its **FOREHEAD**.

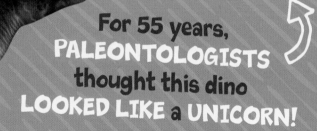

For 55 years, **PALEONTOLOGISTS** thought this dino **LOOKED LIKE** a **UNICORN!**

Then in 2013, a more **COMPLETE SKULL** showed that Tsintaosaurus had a **FAN-SHAPED CREST**, not a **SPIKE**.

MICROPACHYCEPHALOSAURUS

(MY-kro-PACK-ee-SEF-ah-loh-SORE-us)

TIME PERIOD LIVED: LATE CRETACEOUS
70 MILLION YEARS AGO

LOCATION: CHINA

LENGTH: 3.3 FEET (1 M)

MICROPACHYCEPHALOSAURUS
WAS SMALL ...

... BUT IT
WAS GIVEN THE
LONGEST NAME
OF ANY DINOSAUR.

Pachycephalosaurus means "THICK-HEADED LIZARD".

The dome on its SKULL was SOLID BONE— 10 inches (25 cm) thick!

PACHYCEPHALOSAURUS
(pack-ee-SEF-ah-loh-SORE-us)

TIME PERIOD LIVED: LATE CRETACEOUS
65 MILLION YEARS AGO

LOCATION: SOUTH DAKOTA, MONTANA, AND WYOMING, USA

LENGTH: 26 FEET (8 M)

ARCHAEOCERATOPS

(ark-ee-oh-SER-ah-tops)

TIME PERIOD LIVED: MIDDLE CRETACEOUS 99 MILLION YEARS AGO

LOCATION: CHINA

LENGTH: 4.3 FEET (1.3 M)

Archaeoceratops was one of the **EARLIEST "HORNED DINOSAURS"**—except it **DIDN'T HAVE ANY HORNS!**

IT HAD A LARGE HEAD WITH A BEAK AND A FRILL, AND IT WALKED ON TWO LEGS INSTEAD OF FOUR.

MONTANACERATOPS

(mon-TAN-ah-SER-ah-tops)

TIME PERIOD LIVED: LATE TRIASSIC 228 MILLION YEARS AGO

LOCATION: MONTANA, USA, AND CANADA

LENGTH: 10 FEET (3 M)

For decades, scientists thought Montanaceratops had a **SMALL HORN** on its **NOSE**.

THEN THEY REALIZED THE "HORN" WAS REALLY PART OF THE DINOSAUR'S CHEEK!

NEDOCERATOPS

 (NED-oh-SER-ah-tops)

**TIME PERIOD LIVED: LATE CRETACEOUS
70 MILLION YEARS AGO**

LOCATION: WYOMING, USA

LENGTH: 23 FEET (7 M)

NEDOCERATOPS IS ON ITS THIRD NAME!

HELLO
MY NAME IS

NEDOCERATOPS

1. WHEN IT WAS FIRST DISCOVERED, IT WAS NAMED DICERATOPS.

2. THEN FOR A LONG TIME, SCIENTISTS THOUGHT IT WAS JUST AN UNUSUAL TRICERATOPS.

3. FINALLY, IN 2007 IT WAS GIVEN THE NEW NAME, NEDOCERATOPS.

PACHYRHINOSAURUS

(PACK-ee-RHINE-oh-sore-us)

TIME PERIOD LIVED: LATE CRETACEOUS
70 MILLION YEARS AGO

LOCATION: ALASKA, USA, AND CANADA

LENGTH: 20 FEET (6 M)

PALEONTOLOGISTS HAVE FOUND BONEBEDS WITH THOUSANDS OF PACHYRHINOSAURUS FOSSILS.

THESE FOSSILS SHOW THAT PACHYRHINOSAURUS LIVED IN BIG HERDS, JUST LIKE BISON AND WILDEBEEST TODAY.

PROTOCERATOPS

 (pro-toh-SER-ah-tops)

TIME PERIOD LIVED: LATE CRETACEOUS 70 MILLION YEARS AGO

LOCATION: ASIA

LENGTH: 5.9 FEET (1.8 M)

Scientists KNOW MORE about Protoceratops than almost ANY OTHER DINOSAUR.

Nests full of babies show that PROTOCERATOPS PARENTS CARED FOR THEIR YOUNG.

STYRACOSAURUS

(sty-RACK-oh-sore-us)

Styracosaurus had a **FAN** of **SPIKES** on the back of its **FRILL**.

A LARGE HORN STUCK OUT FROM ITS NOSE.

TOROSAURUS

 (tor-oh-SORE-us)

TIME PERIOD LIVED: LATE CRETACEOUS
66 MILLION YEARS AGO

LOCATION: NORTH AMERICA

LENGTH: 25 FEET (7.5 M)

THE **SKULL** OF
TOROSAURUS WAS
9 FEET (2.7 M) LONG!

THAT'S **TWICE AS LONG AS**
THE **SKULL OF A T-REX!**

TRICERATOPS

(tri-SER-ah-tops)

TIME PERIOD LIVED: LATE CRETACEOUS 70 MILLION YEARS AGO

LOCATION: NORTH AMERICA

LENGTH: 30 FEET (9 M)

MANY TRICERATOPS SKULLS HAVE **HEALED WOUNDS** ON THEIR **FRILLS** FROM OTHER TRICERATOPS.

Just like **MODERN SHEEP, ANTELOPE,** and **BISON,** these dinosaurs used their horns to fight!

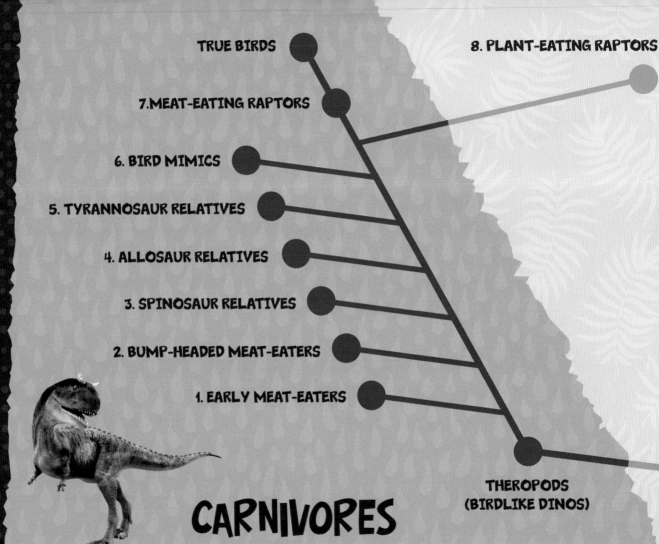

TRUE BIRDS

7. MEAT-EATING RAPTORS

8. PLANT-EATING RAPTORS

6. BIRD MIMICS

5. TYRANNOSAUR RELATIVES

4. ALLOSAUR RELATIVES

3. SPINOSAUR RELATIVES

2. BUMP-HEADED MEAT-EATERS

1. EARLY MEAT-EATERS

THEROPODS
(BIRDLIKE DINOS)

CARNIVORES

HERBIVORES

11. TITANOSAURUS

10. GIANT LONG-NECKS

9. EARLY LONG-NECKS

17. HORNED DINOSAURS

16. BONE-HEADS

15. DUCKBILLS

14. BIRD-FOOTED

13. ARMORED DINOSAURS

12. PLATED DINOSAURS

ORNITHISCHIANS
(BIRD-HIPPED DINOS)

SAURISCHANS
(LIZARD-HIPPED DINOSAURS)

DINOSAURS

	MEAT-EATERS	MEAT-EATERS	RELATIVES	RELATIVES	RELATIVES	6. BIRD-MIMICS	RAPTORS	RAPTORS
LATE TRIASSIC	Coelophysis Eoraptor Herrerasaurus Liliensternus							
EARLY JURASSIC				Cryolophosaurus				
MIDDLE JURASSIC								
LATE JURASSIC				Allosaurus	Coelurus Compsognathus Guanlong			
EARLY CRETACEOUS			Baryonyx Suchomimus	Acrocanthosaurus Neovenator	Eotyrannus		Deinonychus Microraptor Yaverlandia	Beipiaosaurus Caudipteryx Falcarius Incisivosaurus Protarchaeopteryx
MIDDLE CRETACEOUS		Rugops	Spinosaurus	Carcharodontosaurus Giganotosaurus				
LATE CRETACEOUS		Carnotaurus Dahalokely Masiakasaurus			Albertosaurus Alioramus Daspletosaurus Tyrannosaurus rex	Deinocheirus Gallimimus Ornithomimus Shuvuuia	Bambiraptor Buitreraptor Troodon Velociraptor	Avimimus Therizinosaurus

9. EARLY LONG-NECKS	10. GIANT LONG-NECKS	11. TITANOSAURS	12. PLATED DINOSAURS	13. ARMORED DINOSAURS	14. BIRD-FOOT DINOSAURS	15. DUCKBILLS	16. BONE-HEADS	17. HORNED DINOSAURS
Efraasia Plateosaurus Saturnalia Thecodontosaurus								
				Scutellosaurus				
			Huayangosaurus Lexovisaurus					
	Apatosaurus Brachiosaurus Brachytrachelopan Camarasaurus Diplodocus Omeisaurus Suuwassea		Gigantspinosaurus Hesperosaurus Kentrosaurus Stegosaurus Tuojiangosaurus Yingshanosaurus					
				Gastonia Minmi Polacanthus	Hypsilophodon Iguanodon Leaellynasaura Muttaburrasaurus			
		Argentinosaurus Paralititan		Pawpawsaurus	Oryctodromeus			Archaeoceratops
	Huabeisaurus	Ampelosaurus Futalognkosaurus Magyarosaurus Saltasaurus		Aletopelta Ankylosaurus Edmontonia Euoplocephalus Struthiosaurus	Gasparinisaura	Edmontosaurus Hadrosaurus Maiasaura Saurolophus Shantungosaurus Tsintaosaurus	Micropachycephalo- saurus Pachycephalosaurus	Montanaceratops Nedoceratops Pachyrhinosaurus Protoceratops Styracosaurus Torosaurus Triceratops

GLOSSARY

attract—to get the attention of someone or something

burrow—a hole in the ground made or used by an animal

combat—fighting

crest—a curved shape that sticks up from a dinosaur's head

decade—period of ten years

domed—rounded on top

fossil—the remains or traces of an animal or plant, preserved as rock

herd—a large group of animals that lives or moved together

hollow—empty on the inside

keratin—the hard substance that forms hair and fingernails; dinosaur plates were also made of keratin

modern—up-to-date or new

navigate—to steer a course

paleontologist—scientist who studies fossils

plate—flat, bony growth

pompadour—hairstyle in which the hair is combed into a high mound in front

predator—animal that hunts other animals for food

preserve—to protect something so it stays in its original state

sail—tall, thin, upright structure on the backs of some dinosaurs

spine—hard, sharp, pointed growth

READ MORE

Dinosaurs: A Visual Encyclopedia. New York: DK Publishing, 2013.

Holtz, Thomas R., Jr., PhD. *Digging for Tyannosaurus Rex.* Smithsonian: A Discovery Timeline. North Mankato, Minn.: Capstone Press, 2015.

Lessem, Don. *Ultimate Dinopedia: The Most Complete Dinosaur Reference Ever.* National Geographic Kids. Washington, D.C.: National Geographic, 2017.

INTERNET SITES

FactHound offers a safe, fun way to find Internet sites related to this book. All of the sites on FactHound have been researched by our staff.

Here's all you do:

Visit *www.facthound.com*

Type in this code: 9781543529265

INDEX

Mind Benders are published by Capstone,
1710 Roe Crest Drive, North Mankato, Minnesota 56003
www.capstonepub.com

Library of Congress Cataloging-in-Publication Data

Names: Wedel, Mathew J., author.
Title: Totally amazing facts about dinosaurs / by Mathew J. Wedel.
Description: North Mankato, Minnesota : an imprint of Capstone Press,
[2019]
  | Series: Mind benders | Audience: Age 8–11.
Identifiers: LCCN 2018011012 (print) | LCCN 2018017110 (ebook) | ISBN
  9781543529340 (eBook PDF) | ISBN 9781543529265 (hardcover) | ISBN
  9781543529302 (paperback)
Subjects: LCSH: Dinosaurs—Juvenile literature.
Classification: LCC QE861.5 (ebook) | LCC QE861.5 .W3547 2019 (print) |
DDC
  567.9—dc23
LC record available at https://lccn.loc.gov/2018011012